The Energy Crisis
Michael Gibson

THE ENERGY CRISIS

Michael Gibson

Rourke Enterprises, Inc.
Vero Beach, FL 32964

World Issues

Food or Famine?
Nuclear Weapons
Population Growth
The Energy Crisis

Frontispiece: Oil refinery
Cover: Oil rig

First published in the
United States in 1987 by
Rourke Enterprises, Inc.
Vero Beach, FL 32964

Text © 1987 Rourke Enterprises, Inc.

Library of Congress Cataloging-in-Publication Data
Gibson, Michael, 1942-
   The energy crisis.

   (World issues)
   Includes index.
   Summary: Examines the inadequacy of America's
supply of energy resources, the political and economic
ratifications of a growing dependency on foreign
countries for energy, and the problem of developing
new sources of energy while protecting the
environment.
   1. Energy policy – Juvenile literature. 2. Energy
industries – Juvenile literature. 3. Power resources –
Juvenile literature. 4. Renewable energy sources –
Juvenile literature. [1. Energy policy. 2. Energy
industries. 3. Power resources. 4. Renewable energy
sources] I. Title.   II. Series: World issues
HD9502.A2G525   1987   333.79   87–12768
ISBN 0–86592–277–2

Phototypeset by Kalligraphics Ltd., Redhill, Surrey
Printed in Italy by Sagdos S.p.A., Milan

Contents

1 Introduction

Is there an energy crisis?

Energy is the basis of all life and is derived from the sun. Sunlight enables plants to grow and provides animals and human beings with food. Over vast periods of time, heat and pressure have transformed deposits of dead plant and animal matter into fossil fuels such as oil, natural gas and coal. When these fossil fuels are burned, the stored energy that they contain is released. Gradually, human beings have adapted these different forms of energy to help them create a more comfortable environment and to make tools and machines.

Is the world running out of energy? Technically, the answer is no. We will always have sources of "renewable" energy – the sun, human labor and animal power. The sun should continue to supply us with heat and light for many millions of years to come. There is no reason why human beings should not continue tilling the land and breeding animals for food and to provide simple forms of energy.

If this is true, why are so many people worried about our energy supplies? The main reason is that we are rapidly using up our reserves of fossil fuels, the supply of which is obviously limited. Is there anything we can do to slow down this process? Naturally, we could conserve our resources by cutting down on waste, for example, by designing smaller cars that require less gas and oil, building homes that are well insulated and factories that use electricity, gas and oil more efficiently in their manufacturing processes. Indeed, since the

The ultimate source of all our energy is the sun. Its energy derives from the fusion of hydrogen nuclei.

THE NUCLEAR-FREE FUTURE STARTS HERE

introduction of energy conservation policies in the West, consumption has been reduced to such an extent that we use little more now than we did in the early 1970s. And there are others forms of renewable energy that we have yet to exploit on a large scale – ocean currents, tides and solar and wind power.

If there is an energy crisis today, it lies in the Developing World (the countries of South and Southeast Asia, Africa and Latin America). These countries, which only use between 10 and 20 percent of the commercial energy consumed in the West, continue to rely on traditional "renewable" sources of energy. Between one-half and three-quarters of all the energy used comes from crop wastes, animal dung, charcoal and firewood. Over two billion people cook their meals with these fuels. The major

These demonstrators in London, England believe that the hazards of nuclear power outweigh its benefits.

problem now is that large-scale deforestation, caused by the constant demand for firewood, is occurring at a rate that cannot be sustained. This is threatening to disrupt the delicate ecological balance and, among other things, is leading to soil erosion and the loss of much-needed fertile land.

At one time, nuclear power – energy created by the splitting of the atom – seemed to promise a relatively inexpensive means of meeting the world's energy needs. But enthusiasm has cooled somewhat in the wake of the "meltdown" at the Three Mile Island nuclear plant in the U.S. and the explosion at Chernobyl in the

7

U.S.S.R. Growing fears about the consequences of such accidents, combined with increased resistance to the disposal of radioactive waste byproducts, have brought the question of future energy policies into the open once more.

In Tunisia, women still rely on animal power to plow their fields.

The power of energy

Throughout the course of recorded history, the discovery and application of new energy sources have had a profound effect upon the quality of human life. Although by no means the sole influence on our development, energy production has played a vital part in the way society has been organized.

During the Stone Age, the main sources of energy were the sun and human labor. Men and women lived by hunting animals and eating plants. To keep warm they burned natural vegetation. In about 10,000 B.C., people began to cultivate the soil and to keep animals, altering their lifestyle from a nomadic way of life to settled, communal activity. Animals were used to draw vehicles and to pull simple forms of farming equipment, such as plows.

Gradually, humankind learned to exploit natural forms of energy, particularly wind power, for a variety of purposes, for example, sailing ships, watermills and windmills. It was the invention of the steam engine, however, that proved to be one of the most significant developments in the use of energy. Steam-powered machines could perform many tasks more quickly, cheaply and efficiently than human labor. An Industrial Revolution followed, the effects of which were dramatic. Society was transformed within a few decades. The traditional ties with the land and the dependence upon an agricultural economy were rapidly lost as people moved to the cities and to the new industrial towns to find work in factories. A new class system emerged, based upon the divisions of labor created by industrialism. Here was the most potent example of how the utilization of energy has the power to transform the way we live.

The exploitation of fossil fuels – coal, oil and gas – has literally fueled the enormous increase in general living standards in the West over the

Cotton factory in England, 1835. Before the invention of the steam engine, textiles were produced on hand-powered looms in people's homes.

Oil and coal will not run out, but the ratio of energy found to energy spent in obtaining them will continue to increase until costs exceed yields. If the net yield of potential energy begins to approach that of wood, we will have returned to the solar-energy-based economy and by that time the standards of living of the world will have retrogressed to those of two centuries ago. Whether such changes will come suddenly in a catastrophe, or slowly as a gradual trend, is one of the great issues of our time.
Howard T. Odum: Environment, Power and Society

past 100 years. Existing forms of energy have been tailored (or converted, as in the case of electricity produced by coal- and oil-fired power stations) to make available a wide range of labor-saving devices. The only dark cloud on the horizon has been the prospect of the eventual exhaustion of the world's fossil fuel reserves.

What does the future hold? Will society have to change to accommodate new forms of energy or can we adapt our traditional sources to our future needs?

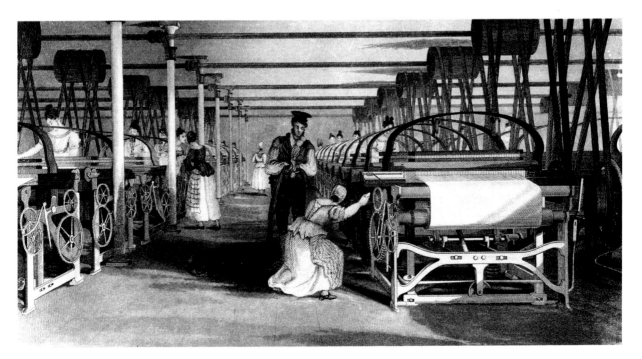

2 Sources of energy

The traditional shape of this seventeenth-century windmill has been replaced by more efficient designs.

Sun and wind

The sun is the ultimate source of all the world's energy. Changes in the angle of the earth's axis, its tilt toward or away from the sun, have a tremendous effect upon climate. The sun is the origin of the world's air and sea currents, its winds and rains.

As long ago as the twelfth century, windmills were used to grind corn and to pump water. These windmills were powered by four or six giant sails that were thirty feet or more in length. To keep the mill facing the wind, the entire tower (or the dome to which the sails were attached) was rotated. This was either done by hand or sometimes by a rudder or vane fixed at right angles to the sails, which automatically shifted the dome when the wind veered.

Windmills are still in use in many parts of the world today. In fact, giant mills are under construction to see if they have a viable role to play in the production of electricity. In

October 1986, the first full-sized wind turbine began operating in Carmarthen Bay, South Wales. The 130-kilowatt machine is expected to contribute to Britain's electricity supply network. At rest, its blades look like huge football posts, but when spinning at top speed they tilt until they form an arrowhead shape.

The Department of Energy in Britain is considering constructing a number of wind "farms" at Richborough in Kent, the Scilly Isles and the Orkneys. It believes that a small "farm" of ten windmills will produce power at a rate comparable to other energy sources. For this reason, wind power is widely regarded as one of the most promising of the "renewables."

The introduction of the windmill as a prime-mover did not proceed smoothly. The craftsmen's guilds of Holland protested against them in 1591, claiming they would throw many craftsmen out of work. A mechanical saw worked by a windmill was built in 1766 at Limehouse, east of London, but was destroyed by a riotous mob two years later.

History of Technology

Wind farms may become a familiar sight on hilltops in the future.

The biomass

The biomass is the living weight of the organisms at different levels of the food chain. The food chain may be thought of as forming a pyramid, the base consisting of a great mass of primary consumers (e.g. plants – insects – birds) and the apex of the relatively few ultimate consumers (humans). The number of individuals in a food chain decreases at each succeeding level, while the size of the individual tends to increase.

Green plants collect solar energy and use it in a process called photosynthesis, which produces carbohydrates. This energy is used mostly for growth, but some is stored. When animals or humans eat these plants, they are able to absorb this stored energy, which enables them in turn to grow and function. This energy is passed along the food chain to its peak, providing each of us with our individual daily energy requirements.

Below During photosynthesis, a plant absorbs water and carbon dioxide and uses solar energy to convert them to oxygen and glucose.

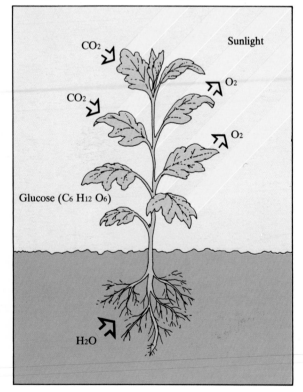

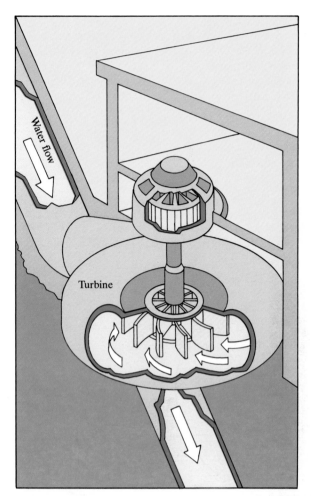

Above This turbine coverts the kinetic energy of flowing water to electrical energy.

Hydropower

The energy of fast-flowing water has been exploited since ancient times. Water wheels were used to grind corn and to work other machines. The water wheel in its traditional form, however, proved too inefficient and unwieldy. Then, in the nineteenth century, the reaction turbine was developed. This forced water through a curved casing containing a vaned wheel. Turbines of this kind are used with great success by electricity plants on the Yenisey River in Siberia and on the Churchill Falls in Canada.

However, the full potential of the world's rivers has yet to be tapped. As a steady flow of water is required for maximum efficiency, rivers are often dammed flooding large areas. The Cabora Dassa project in Mozambique, for example, has a lake 155 miles long covering an area of 1,042 square miles. High evaporation rates are a problem. Moreover, reservoirs gradually silt up, with some areas becoming swamps and mudflats. Unless these reservoirs can be flushed clear of silt, the power stations they feed will eventually be starved of water and cease to be effective.

The creation of such dams and reservoirs is often controversial. Quite frequently, they require the flooding of large tracts of agricultural land and the compulsory movement and resettlement of the original inhabitants. So far South America, Africa and Southeast Asia have exploited only 20 percent of their potential

Large hydroelectric projects, like this one on Snake River, disrupt their immediate environment, but produce no pollution.

Unfortunately, the battery-powered cars that have been produced so far are suitable only for very short journeys.

hydroelectric resources. The Inga River in the Congo, for instance, has a generating capacity of 25,000 megawatts, while the Bramaputra in India could produce 20,000 megawatts.

At present, the world's hydroelectric stations are producing 322,000 megawatts, some 16 percent of possible output. It is unlikely, however, that world hydro resources will ever be fully exploited, because water is needed for all kinds of other purposes such as irrigation, transportation and fishing.

Electricity storage

Although most traditional fuels like coal and oil can be stored without difficulty, electricity cannot. In order to solve the problems caused by variations in its production and consumption, it must be converted into other forms of energy. The most common method is "pump storage." During periods of low demand, electricity is used to pump water from a low-lying lake or reservoir to one higher up. When the demand for electricity rises, the water in the upper reservoir is released and passes through turbo-generators on its way back to the lower lake, thereby creating electricity.

Another method is compressed air storage. Surplus electricity is used to compress air and store it under pressure in underground reservoirs. When demand increases, the air is allowed to expand, powering generators that produce electricity. Experiments are also being carried out to investigate the possibility of storing electricity in superconductors. In theory, copper coils at a temperature of minus 270°C can be charged or discharged to store or release electricity as required.

Batteries are by far the commonest form of storage, although at present they can only be used to power small-scale operations. Battery operated vehicles, for instance, usually have a strictly limited range. Nevertheless, scientists are continually seeking to produce super-batteries that could be used for long periods.

Attempts are also being made to utilize hydrogen gas as a fuel. When the gas is burned in the air it produces water, not poisonous waste, so that it is pollution free. In the United States, hydrogen fuel cells are being built as alternatives to normal power stations. The cells generate electricity from hydrogen-rich gas and the only waste that is produced is hot air, which can be released straight into the atmosphere.

The storage of electricity remains a problem, as such "solutions" as have been found so far are "very naive and expensive."

Coal

Coal has been used as a form of fuel from early Roman times. It played a great part in the Industrial Revolution and remained the chief source of energy in the West until the 1950s when oil supplanted it. Now, it seems, coal is about to make a comeback.

Whereas oil and natural gas reserves are limited to fulfilling only short-term energy needs, there are at least 750 billion tons of coal available to be mined. In other words, it is reasonable to expect that coal will still be in widespread use in 200 years time. This is just as well, as experts predict that coal may have to supply between one-half and two-thirds of the world's additional fuel requirements over the next twenty years. Although 80 percent of

Most of the coal that we use is mined underground. Extracting it is a dirty and dangerous job.

currently known coal reserves are in the United States, the U.S.S.R. and China, there are also rich, untapped seams in many developing countries. To meet the predicted levels of future energy consumption, however, world coal production would have to be doubled.

Although coal is not as versatile a fuel as oil or natural gas, it can be used to produce electricity, or processed to yield byproducts such as gas, oil and a wide variety of chemicals.

Efforts are being made to discover efficient ways of converting coal into gas while it is still in the ground.

Liquid synthetic fuels of various kinds can be made from coal. During the Second World War, the Germans produced fuels from coal not only for motorized transportation but for the world's first jet fighters. The South Africans also convert coal into oil substitutes. However, conversion is expensive and it is cheaper and easier to use oil as long as reserves last.

Coal is also used to make plastics including nylon, photographic materials, drugs such as aspirin, disinfectants, fertilizers, paints, varnishes and even perfumes. In Victorian times, coal was so highly valued that it became known as "black diamonds." Changing patterns of energy production and consumption in the future may well return it to its former preeminence.

Oil and natural gas

Since the 1950s, oil has been the main source of the world's commercial energy. It also comprises one-eighth of the world's trade. Eighty-five percent of this oil is consumed by the richer, industrialized countries in the world. However, developing countries are also heavily dependent on oil. It accounts for 75 percent of the commercial energy they use. In 1981, the President of Kenya, Daniel Arap-t-moi, pointed out that many poor countries have to spend 50 percent of their foreign exchange earnings on oil imports. Why is oil so important?

Oil is a very versatile substance, which provides gasoline for cars; petroleum gas for

Plastic goods like these are only a few of the many items made from oil.

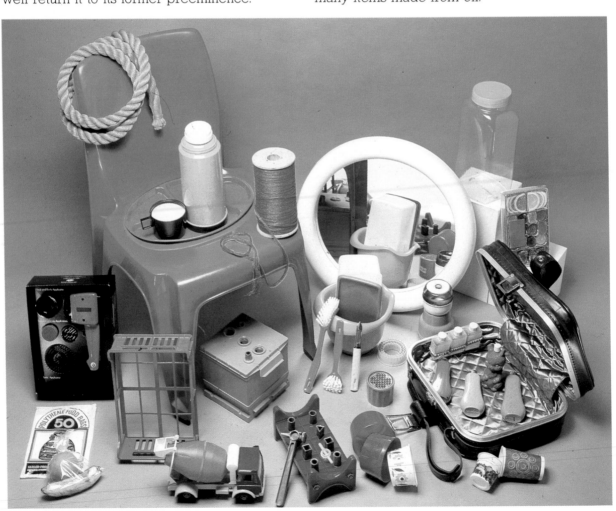

Laying gas pipes. A large expenditure on infra-structure is needed to develop a gas industry.

stoves; naphtha, which can be converted into nylon, PVC plastics and synthetic rubber; kerosene, which is used for domestic heating and aviation oil; and gas oil, which can fuel domestic heating systems and power stations, as well as provide protein food for animals.

The versatility of oil has made it an invaluable commodity, but reserves are limited. Conservation and energy-saving policies have slowed consumption significantly, but there is still an urgent need to develop other resources. Oil

17

shales and tar sands have great potential, but are difficult and expensive to process. There are already a few shale-oil industries in Scotland, Sweden, France and China. Vast deposits of tar sands are available in Canada, the United States, Madagascar and Venezuela. With improved technology, it is hoped to make much greater use of these resources.

It is thought that there are more oil and gas reserves still to be discovered in the developing countries, which have as yet not been fully explored. One form of energy that is being more widely used is natural gas, which now provides 20 percent of the world's total energy needs. Over 75 percent of the known gas reserves are in North America, the Middle East, the U.S.S.R. and China. Few developing countries have built up their own gas industries since their domestic demand has generally been too small to justify building the necessary pipelines. However, this is likely to change in the future. Gas is a very convenient fuel and a survey of the developing countries suggests that it could supply 10–15 percent of their total commercial energy needs by 1990.

It is hoped that our dependence on oil will gradually lessen as more fuel substitutes are developed. The exploitation of natural gas may provide part of the solution to the oil crisis.

Nuclear energy

As we have seen, the world's reserves of oil, gas and coal can provide an adequate energy supply for only a limited period of time. The renewable sources of energy – the sun, wind, rivers, tides and waves – will always be there, but at the moment we do not have the means to use them on a large scale. It is feared that, in the future, an energy gap may emerge when fossil fuels will no longer supply all our needs and we will not be able to rely on renewable sources of energy to take their place. At one time, it seemed that nuclear energy would provide the ideal way to fill this gap.

A nuclear power station is very like an oil- or coal-fired station. Heat is used to boil water, which produces steam. The steam turns a huge turbine and this produces electricity. The difference is that a nuclear power station uses heat energy released by splitting atoms of uranium. This process is controlled by rods or "moderators" made out of boron and graphite, which ensure that the reaction continues at a manageable level. Splitting uranium atoms releases many times more energy than burning the same weight of oil. A ton of uranium used in a nuclear power station can produce as much energy as 25,000 tons of coal.

There are, however, two drawbacks to nuclear power. The first is the radioactive waste that is produced during the production process. Although this accounts for only 0.3 percent of the uranium used, its disposal poses serious

A nuclear fission chain reaction. This process is carefully controlled in a nuclear reactor; uncontrolled fission takes place in a nuclear bomb.

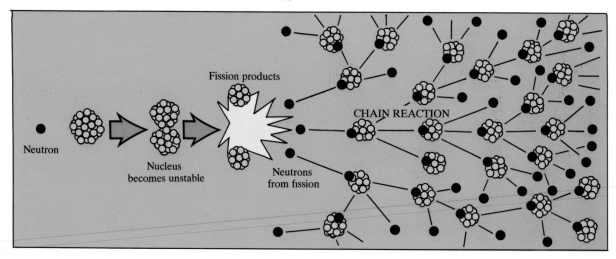

Neutron

Nucleus becomes unstable

Fission products

Neutrons from fission

CHAIN REACTION

problems as the radioactivity can take hundreds of years to decay. The waste material is usually buried in secure casks deep under ground, but many people are very concerned about the risks to the environment should leak occur. The second problem with nuclear power is the possibility of an accident occurring at a power station, as happened at Three Mile Island in 1979 and Chernobyl in 1986 (see page 28). The radioactivity that is released during such an accident cannot be confined to a particular area. It recognizes no geographical or political boundaries. The extend of its spread is determined entirely by the prevailing weather conditions; therefore, any such leakage immediately becomes an international problem.

Such incidents have tended to dampen enthusiasm for the nuclear solution to the energy crisis, although there are currently 282 nuclear reactors operating in twenty-five countries. These provide over 50 percent of France's energy requirements, 38 percent of Sweden's, 16 percent of Japan's, 13 percent of the U.S.'s and 6 percent of the U.S.S.R.'s. However, Denmark and Australia have decided not to develop nuclear power at all, and Sweden is phasing out its own plants. Many European countries are also reconsidering their own policies in the wake of Chernobyl.

The risks to workers and the general public from the nuclear industry are low. However, the consequences of a single accident could be so catastrophic that there is considerable debate as to whether it is safe to continue producing energy in this way,.

Several countries dump some of their nuclear waste at sea although this is bitterly opposed by environmentalists.

3
The problems of energy

Energy policy and politics

Today, we live in an interdependent world. Countries buy and sell a wide range of goods and commodities, both to make money and to create or cement political alliances. Energy is part of this process. Commodities such as oil, coal and uranium are bought and sold on the international markets in deals worth millions of dollars. This economic importance gives energy political power too – it can be used as an economic weapon and as a political tool. The most potent example of this occurred in 1973, when war broke out in the Middle East between Egypt and Israel. The Arab oil-producing countries (Iran, Iraq, Qatar, Saudi Arabia, the United Arab Emirates and Libya) deliberately reduced their collective output and cut off supplies to those countries that traditionally supported the Israelis. Oil, upon which the world is so dependent, quadrupled in price in a matter of weeks causing widespread economic problems in the West and in the countries of the Developing World. In the West, inflation rates soared and industrial productivity was threatened as factories strove to conserve or cut back energy consumption. In the Developing World, the blow was just as hard and it had long-term adverse consequences. These countries, their economies already weak, were faced with an enormous increase in their oil import bills. Unable to cope with this sudden increase, they were forced to borrow from Western banks and the International Monetary Fund (IMF). These loans, made under commercial rates, forced crippling repayments on the developing countries for many years. The legacy of the oil crisis therefore remains, condemning these countries to the burden of long-term interest and capital payments. They have become the innocent victims of international power politics.

This political manipulation by the official cartel for oil production, OPEC (the Arab states plus Ecuador, Venezuela, Algeria, Gabon, Nigeria and Indonesia), brought economic rewards too from the sustained increase in prices. However, the stricter conservation policies that resulted, combined with the increased production of the new independent oil-producing states (Norway and Britain, for example) have together diminished OPEC's political and economic power. This, in turn, has

Oil crisis in Britain, 1973. This bank was using as little lighting as possible in an attempt to save energy.

led to overproduction in recent years, causing low prices and severe difficulties for all oil-associated industries.

So, energy production is a business, prone to the booms and slumps of the economic market place. The contrasting fortunes of oil since 1973 provide a graphic example of how fickle the market place can be. This, in turn, makes it problematic for governments and private energy businesses to plan energy supplies and to estimate future income. Short

OPEC ministers meet regularly to set the price of oil and to decide on production quotas.

of an international agreement between the producers and the consumers of oil, fixing a stable price over a definite time period (a development that would remove much political and economic uncertainty), there seems little alternative in prospect to the present unpredictability of the supply of and demand for oil.

In terms of international energy production, there are obviously many conflicts of interest among different countries. However, each country also has its own energy resources and it must decide how it exploits these, a choice that is basically a political one. Should the means of energy production and distribution lie in public or prviate hands. Fossil fuels are arguably a national asset and should not be licensed out for the profit of private individuals. According to this argument, all energy resources should be owned and exploited by the state for the benefit of the people, making only sufficient profits to cover costs and to renew investment. Energy policies would then be dictated by the country's needs, rather than by financial interests alone. However, state-owned industries are prone to domestic political manipulation: for instance, governments can fix prices at a higher level than strictly necessary to cream off extra income, thus creating a form of "invisible taxation."

What about purely private ownership? This would seek to use energy to gain maximum profit for a few individuals (the company shareholders), which might cause the company to ignore wider economic, social and environmental issues in the way it conducts its business. Some people advocate a mixture of public and private ownership, with the government retaining at least 51 percent ownership of a nationalized energy industry (for example, oil or coal) and selling the remainder to private interests. The government can then retain control of the company's overall policies to protect the national interest, while the element of private enterprise would, in theory, encourage the most efficient methods of production and distribution.

Developed countries often provide developing nations with economic and political assistance in tackling energy projects, such as building hydroelectric dams and power stations. Energy here is used not only as a means of securing an economic market for the donor country, but also as a way of winning political influence – exporting ideology with technology. Often these expensive, prestigious projects do not serve the real needs of the recipient nation, but only the minority of the population who live in the major cities.

Energy policies cannot be separated from politics. Governments have to make choices about the types of energy we use and have a responsibility to research into those we might need in the future and the way in which they are to be exploited, taking into account their feasibility, their safety and their cost in financial, environmental and social terms. These decisions arouse deep feelings and provoke intense debate, with beliefs and predictions often counting as much as the facts.

> How much longer should the taxpayer be expected to subsidize uneconomic pits? The coal industry must move with the times – become leaner, fitter, more efficient.
> *Ian McGregor: former Chairman of the British National Coal Board*
>
> We are witnessing the butchering of the coal-mining industry in Britain, whole communities being thrown on the rubbish dump, people being sacrificed on the altar of profit and loss.
> *Arthur Scargill: leader of the National Union of Miners in England*

The North-South divide

In 1980, the Independent Commission on International Development Issues, chaired by Willy Brandt, issued *North-South: A Programme for Survival.* The Brandt Report, as it is called, pointed out the gross inequality existing between the developed industrial countries of the Northern Hemisphere and the poorer developing countries of the Southern Hemisphere. "One American uses as much commercial energy as two Germans or Australians, three Swiss or Japanese, six Yugoslavs, nine Mexicans or Cubans, sixteen Chinese, nineteen Malaysians, fifty-three Indians or Indonesians, 109 Sri Lankans, 438 Malians or 1072 Nepalese."

Developing countries are largely dependent on traditional energy sources, such as

This vast oil refinery is owned by Shell – one of the seven companies that dominate the world oil trade.

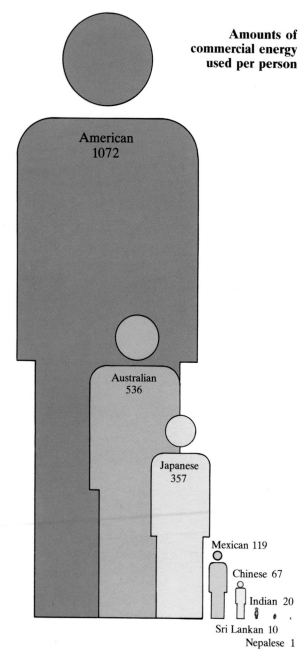

Amounts of commercial energy used per person

American 1072

Australian 536

Japanese 357

Mexican 119

Chinese 67

Indian 20

Sri Lankan 10

Nepalese 1

Comparison of energy consumption (arbitrary units). Energy is even more unequally distributed between rich and poor countries than food.

human and animal power, firewood and animal dung, while the industrialized countries utilize oil, natural gas, coal and nuclear energy. Even though the industrialized North has only a quarter of the world's population, it accounts for more than half the world's energy consumption.

For the rest of the century, oil, natural gas and other non-renewable sources of energy will have to supply the majority of the world's needs. The Brandt Report, however, called for fuller exploitation of renewable sources like wind, solar and geothermal energy, hydropower and ocean energy as well as realizing the potential of oil shale and tar sand deposits. The authors of the report also recommended the creation of a global energy research center under the supervision of the United Nations: "Such a center could support, in particular, research in the field of renewable sources of energy."

The Brandt Report further suggests that "the industrial countries will have to alter lifestyles they have based on abundant energy if they are not to suffer an energy crisis or consume more than their fair share of the world's resources." The report's authors believe the poor countries have a right to a larger share of the world's energy resources so that they can raise their people's standard of living.

During the last half century, the demand for commercial energy has increased sixfold. While, in years to come, the developed countries will continue to consume large quantities of energy, the consumption of the developing countries will grow at a much faster rate. One of the most important questions facing the world is how we are to satisfy the needs of both groups of countries fairly.

The silent spring

The production of most forms of energy causes pollution. The oil industry, for instance, often experiences difficulties. Wells "blow out," pipelines burst and oil tankers sink. In 1967, in perhaps the most infamous accident, the *Torrey Canyon* ran aground off the coast of Cornwall, England, and the consequent oil slick caused widespread pollution of the coast and brought a slow and painful death to many thousands of seabirds, fish and other forms of sea and seashore life.

The exhaust fumes produced by cars are also a major health hazard. The internal combustion engine is not only noisy and inefficient, but the gases it produces are potentially lethal.

It is feared that toxic proportions of lead and nickel are slowly building up in the atmosphere and many governments have passed legislation to make their oil industries reduce the quantity of metals in their gasoline.

Coal is another major source of air pollution.

Many large, industrial cities suffer from terrible "smogs" in winter, when temperature inversions trap layers of grime-filled air over them,

This gray seal has been killed by oil pollution.

sometimes for days on end. Britain has largely overcome this problem thanks to the Clean Air Act of 1956, which required householders and factory owners to use "smokeless" fuels such as anthracite.

Burning coal emits sulfur oxides, heavy metals (lead, mercury and cadmium), radioactive elements (such as radium and uranium), hydrocarbons and large quantities of carbon

A Senate committee investigating the effect of man-made pollutants on the atmosphere was told that temperatures could rise within only 15 years "to a level which has not existed on earth in the past 100,000 years." Scientists fear that the "greenhouse effect" caused by pollution will cause melting of polar ice caps, floods, drought and more skin disease.
Newspaper report, June 1986

The lead in car exhaust fumes is throught to be particularly damaging to children's health.

dioxide. The increase in carbon dioxide in the atmosphere is potentially a serious danger, as it causes heat to be trapped there. Some experts fear that unless this trend can be reversed, a "greenhouse" condition could result which would cause a long-term change in climate leading eventually to the Polar ice caps melting and flooding much of the present land mass. A far more immediate danger is the release into the atmosphere of sulfur and nitrogen oxides from burning coal. Some of those oxides fall as gas in the local area, corroding metals and buildings. Most, however, combine with water vapor in the atmosphere to form acids that are deposited by rainfall over distances of hundreds of miles. This seriously damages natural vegetation and all the life forms that depend upon it. Acid rain has caused many problems in Europe, particularly in Sweden, Norway, Austria, Switzerland and West Germany. Many Western European nations have taken steps to reduce harmful emissions from power stations, but only by about 30 percent, as this process is relatively expensive.

At one time, environmentalists feared that

Many trees in Europe and North America are dying from the effects of industrial pollution.

uncontrolled pollution would lead to a "silent spring," when no plant would grow and no animal stir. This apocalyptic situation is no longer inevitable. Governments everywhere are introducing or strengthening existing anti-pollution policies. Many people, however, think that such policies should be given higher priority and greater financial support than they receive at present.

The Chernobyl disaster

On April 26, 1986, an accident set the graphite core of a nuclear reactor at Chernobyl, in the Soviet Ukraine, on fire. According to the Soviets, the accident occurred during an experiment to see how long a turbine generator would provide power after losing steam

A helicopter is used to survey the devastated nuclear plant at Chernobyl. The damaged reactor is now encased in steel and concrete.

supplies. The automatic operating and emergency cooling systems were switched off. Power dropped rapidly. When the pumps were turned on, the core reached boiling point. The operators discovered they could not shut down the reactor manually. Steam pressure blew off the top of the reactor, a cloud of hydrogen gas quickly formed and ignited, causing a fire ball to rip through the station. Radioactivity was released into the atmosphere and, for a time, many people feared a total meltdown of the reactor's core. If this had happened, the core might have burned its way right through the earth's crust, leading to the so-called China Syndrome. The courage of the Soviet firemen prevented such a disaster, although many of them lost their lives in the process. Sand, lead, clay, dolomite and boron were thrown on top of the damaged reactor to seal the breach.

Chernobyl was a potent reminder that human beings are fallible; we are prone to error. This means that no matter how theoretically safe the production of nuclear power is, the real question is "how safe is it in our hands?"
Ron Punt: After Chernobyl

The radioactive cloud released from Chernobyl was especially disastrous for the Lapps. Their pastures were so badly contaminated that their reindeer meat is unfit to eat.

Later, the reactor was completely surrounded by a thick wall of concrete.

It seems that the people of the world were lucky on April 26! Lucky that weather conditions were calm and the radioactive cloud was able to rise straight up into the atmosphere, instead of being blown across the surrounding countryside spreading sickness and death. However, it is difficult to regard this disaster calmly. Between thirty and forty people died, 200 more suffered from acute radiation sickness and 135,000 people had to be evacuated from the areas around the plant. Large areas of agricultural land were seriously polluted. As the winds carried the radioactive cloud across Western Europe, few countries escaped the consequences – animals had to be slaughtered, vegetable produce destroyed, radiation levels on land and in lakes measured.

The importance of the Chernobyl disaster lies in what lessons the people of the world draw from it. In many countries the immediate reaction has been to halt or slow down the construction of reactors. The greater the number of reactors, the bigger the chance of a disaster occurring. On the other hand, can we afford to ignore such a promising source of energy at a time when supplies of traditional fuels are running down?

4
The future of energy

Conservation

It has been suggested that the developed countries should cut their energy consumption by building fewer roads, houses and factories. However, this type of policy affects a country's economic growth and this can have unwanted side effects, such as an increase in unemployment. This, in turn, leads to a fall in demand for consumer goods because people have less money to spend and the rate of decline accelerates. To counter this, some economists have promoted the idea of a "steady-state economy"

– one with zero economic growth. Are such drastic methods necessary? Conservation policies may produce the required effect without such a massive upheaval.

Modern society no longer squanders resources at the rate that it did twenty years ago. We are saving energy by building smaller cars that have higher compression ratios, better ignition control, leaner gasoline-air mixtures and improved transmission systems. The American government, for instance, has introduced legislation to cut car fuel consumption by half over the next twenty years. This, however, has had drastic implications for the domestic oil industry, which is suffering financially from the reduced level of demand.

Domestic energy consumption in the United States and Western Europe totals between 30 and 40 percent of their respective national energy requirements. Three-quarters of this domestic consumption is used for heating and

This diagram shows the distribution of heat losses from a typical home.

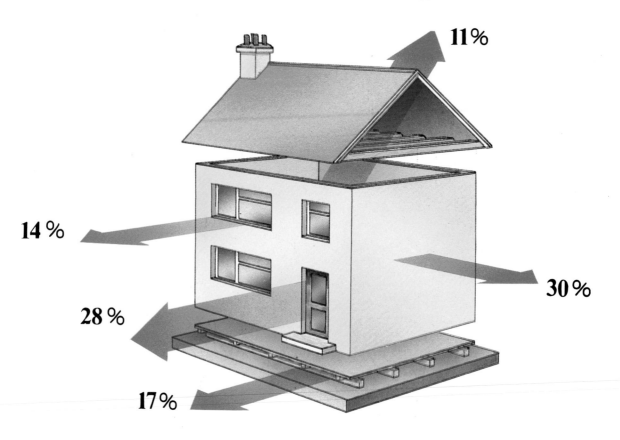

11%

14%

30%

28%

17%

__Above__ Home insulation is a very cost-effective way of reducing domestic energy consumption.

cooling buildings, the rest on lighting, cooking, water heating and powering domestic devices. Water heating uses up about 5–10 percent of a house's total energy consumption. Taking showers instead of baths, fitting spray taps, instead of the normal single nozzle variety and insulating tanks and pipes save significant amounts of energy. Poor building design and inadequate insulation waste vast quantities of energy. Heat is lost through conduction, drafts and deliberate ventilation.

A single glazed window loses heat six times as fast as an insulated cavity wall. Savings of up to 30–50 percent can be achieved by such measures as lowering the amount of heating and improving insulation around windows and doorways and in roofs and walls.

Much is being done to encourage people to improve the insulation of their homes. Policies that offer people tangible advantages, such as improvement grants, are more likely to be effective than moral exhortations to "conserve all you can." The implementation of conservation policies is causing the threat of the energy crisis to recede, in the West at least.

The picture is not so promising in the Developing World, which is facing a growing crisis as supplies of firewood dwindle rapidly. In many countries great areas of forest land have been cut down. In addition to supplying firewood for the local peoples, these forests have a vital ecological role (for example,

Many women in developing countries walk long distances every day to collect firewood.

A firewood crisis is growing as supplies dwindle. In many countries forest land is rapidly turning to desert. Once villagers could find the fuel wood needed close by, but now many must walk far for it ... Deforestation also causes problems of soil erosion ... As fuel wood supplies grow scarce and more expensive, more animal and crop residues are being burnt as fuel. New forests are needed, and more efficient ways of burning wood.

History of Technology

absorbing carbon dioxide and releasing oxygen into the atmosphere; providing a living environment for a wide range of animals and plants; providing nourishment and solidity for the soil). With the trees gones, the vital top soil dries and crumbles so that it is blown away, producing "dust-bowl" conditions. Deforestation is a significant problem in sixty-five countries that suffer from soil erosion. New forests are being planted, but not at a sufficient pace to replace those being destroyed. It is obvious that replanting programs must be increased and that more efficient methods of burning wood (such as "air-tight" stoves) must be introduced to prevent a real energy and ecological crisis occurring.

Sights like this car dump have prompted some commentators to refer to the West as the "throw-away society."

Recycling

Garbage disposal is one of modern society's main problems. On the one hand, worn out articles have to be disposed of, and on the other, they have to be replaced. This represents a double expenditure of energy. Recycling can dramatically reduce this waste. In developed countries, a normal family produces about a ton of garbage a year. Much of this garbage contains valuable raw materials that can be recovered. For many years, scrap metal merchants have carried out a valuable service salvaging anything from tin cans to obsolete battleships. Metals such as steel, copper and tin can be extracted from such waste, then processed and reused to make new items.

Garbage can be used in land reclamation. Old quarries and drained marshes are filled with refuse and then flattened with bulldozers. This, however, can be dangerous. If the garbage is not properly sorted and treated, it can give off poisonous fumes that can make people living close to the site extremely ill. Some garbage (especially paper and food scraps) can be ground up and used as a soil preparation, while animal and human feces can be used as manures in place of expensive artificial fertilizers.

All kinds of processed garbage can add to our energy supplies. Combustible materials can be made into pellets and sold as fuel. Power plants have been developed that burn waste products to produce electricity. Plant, animal and human wastes are used in countries like India to produce biogas, which contains 55–65 percent methane and can be used for lighting and cooking. Specially adapted internal combustion engines can be run on the gas produced by the fermented feces of chickens and other livestock. For thousands of years, animal and human feces have been dried and burned as fuels.

Unfortunately, the collection, sorting and treatment of waste products is energy consuming and expensive. Recycling can save valuable materials, reduce pollution and create fuels and fertilizers. However, it can never play more than a limited role in any energy resource policy.

A biogas digester. Animal wastes can be used either as a fuel or as fertilizers.

Solar energy

At the moment, we can exploit only a fraction of the sun's energy. One of the most promising "high-tech" ways of utilizing this energy source is the photovoltaic collector. Cells of this kind directly transform the sun's rays into electricity.

Photovoltaic cells are a spinoff of space exploration and are used by the space shuttle as a source of power. In fact, they could be employed for all manner of domestic and commercial purposes. In hot climates, for example, they could make homes and factories virtually independent of other energy sources, thereby cutting down the need for traditional fuels.

The world leader in the use of solar energy is California. The state authorities expect to get all the extra electricity they need, as far ahead as the 1990s, from a variety of renewable resources. In fact, their belief is so strong that all nuclear and coal power stations originally planned for construction during this period have now been canceled.

One of the most important methods of achieving this goal will be the increased use of solar

Photovoltaic cells produce electricity directly from sunlight without generating any by-products.

power stations. Typical of the kind of solar power station now being installed in California is the Luz system from Israel. This consists of an array of curved mirrors, which concentrates the sun's rays onto a centrally positioned "collector pipe." Oil flowing through this pipe heats up very quickly and they goes through a heat exchanger, which produces steam at temperatures of 300°C. The steam is then used to drive turbines that generate electricity.

One reason why California is the leader in the field of solar energy is that it gives very generous tax relief to builders of solar power stations. Otherwise, at the present state of development, many solar systems would not be economical. However, significant technological advances are expected over the next few years and the costs of these power stations are expected to fall dramatically by the end of

the 1980s.

In the future, (indeed, some experts would argue, still in the realms of science fiction) are plans to intercept solar energy at full strength in mid-space. Satellites bearing huge collections of solar cells would beam microwaves back to earth to be converted into electricity.

> The proposal that . . . we put up giant satellites to intercept solar energy, convert it there to microwave radiation, beam it to earth in a dilute enough form not to make a death ray of it, reconvert it to electrical energy and then transmit it to our cities appears even less attractive in its long-range possibilities. It is far beyond our present capability except at prohibitive cost.
>
> *H. C. Hattel and J. B. Howard: New Energy Technology*

A solar power plant in California. All of the mirrors focus sunlight onto the central pipe.

At the moment, such schemes are impractical but technological breakthroughs could make them commercially viable in the twenty-first century.

Solar energy, in one form or another, is therefore becoming an important source of power.

Marine power

The ocean could be an endless source of power, but as yet it is one that human beings have had great difficulty in utilizing. Ocean tides, waves, temperature gradients and currents could be exploited to create electricity.

Water covers two-thirds of the earth's surface. For this reason most of the sun's energy reaching the earth is absorbed by the oceans. The Lockheed company in the United States has now developed a practical and exciting method of extracting energy from under the oceans. This is known as OTEC and stands for Ocean Thermal Energy Conversion.

In some parts of the world, such as the Caribbean and large areas of the Pacific Ocean, the water near the surface traps great amounts of solar heat. Much deeper, under these warm layers, the sea temperature is cooler. Lockheed have developed OTEC technology to make use of this temperature difference. A full-scale OTEC plant will be a truly gigantic piece of engineering – at least the size of the largest North Sea oil platforms.

The principle behind an OTEC plant is quite simple. A liquid with a low boiling point (such as ammonia) is used in a closed circuit. Warm surface water turns the liquid to a gas, which expands and drives a turbine to generate electricity (an undersea cable carries this to a nearby city). Once through the turbine, the cooler gas is pumped down to a depth of 2,500 feet where the cooler part of the ocean condenses it back to a liquid state, and the whole cycle starts again.

Lockheed already have a 50-kilowatt prototype in operation off Hawaii in the Pacific. If all the tests are successful, OTECs of up to 2 megawatts will be built – enough to power a city of 20,000 people.

Diagram of an OTEC plant, showing the ammonia circuit. Temperature gradients in the sea are an inexhaustible energy source.

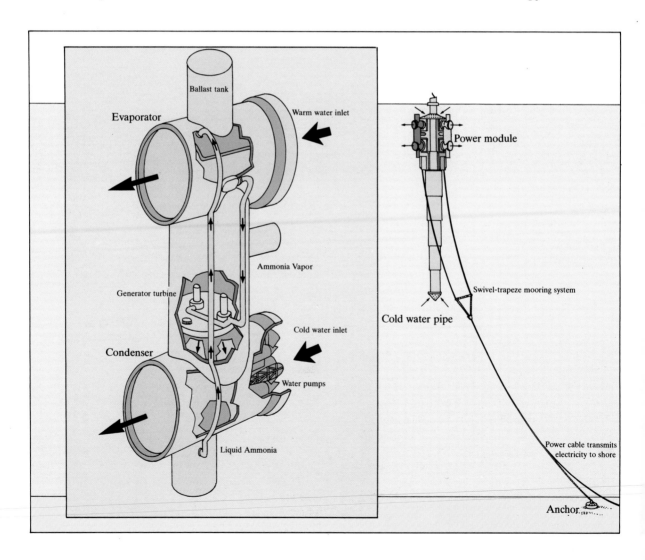

Hot rocks

There are vast quantities of heat stored deep within the earth. The principal cause of this is the decay of radioactive elements in the earth's core, which has a temperature of about 6,000°C. In some parts of the world, due to local geological conditions, some of this heat is near enough to the surface to be used. About eighty countries possess some areas where it would be possible to tap this "geothermal" energy.

Rotorua, New Zealand. Boiling surface pools are heated by geothermal energy.

Geothermal energy can be used in two ways. It can be used directly to heat homes and businesses (space heating) and to provide them with hot water. The earth's heat can also be used for generating electricity, and it is to this use that most attention is being turned.

The dry steam and hot water that rise to the surface can be used to work turbines to generate electricity. Since 1904, the Italians have made use of natural steam in this way at Larderello, while geothermal water is used to heat homes, hospitals and factories at Wairaki in New Zealand. Reykjavik, Iceland's capital, is almost entirely heated by geothermal waters.

A geothermal power plant. Exploitation of this energy source is still at the experimental stage.

Bananas and other tropical fruits are grown in great greenhouses heated in this way and yet Iceland lies on the Arctic Circle! In California, just to the north of San Francisco, a geothermal field powers the turbines of a huge electricity generating station.

The oil crises of the 1970s and 1980s have encouraged research into this energy source. Soon, it is hoped to bore holes through the earth's crust to the hot rocks below. Cold water will be pumped into them where it will be heated and rise up other channels as steam to electricity plants. The life of such a power station would be limited as the rocks would gradually cool down. However, there can be serious disadvantages. The cost of transporting steam and hot water is great; steam is often corrosive and has an appalling smell. Moreover, we do not know how the exploitation of hot rocks would affect the earth's geology. On the other hand, if the steam and hot water could be used to generate electricity on the spot, its transportation would be cheap and easy.

As yet, geothermal sources of energy have hardly been utilized, but with research and new technology it is hoped they will become a major force in the future.

Alternative technology

Some people believe human beings should abandon what they conceive to be "the heavily energy-consumptive, centralized, pollutive, urbanized activity of modern society" in favor of "the minimum environmental interference." Believers in alternative technology hope to free people from what they believe to be the domination of large-scale centralized systems, so that they can concentrate on small-scale operations that focus on the home and simple crafts. In no field is this more true than that of energy. Both its use and its non-use help to increase

Kibbutz Shefef. Israeli kibbutzim are perhaps the best example of small-scale, "decentralized" communities.

ecological stress. We have seen elsewhere some of the problems that energy use creates: acid rain from burning coal; photochemical smogs from vehicle exhausts; radioactive waste from nuclear power stations; and carbon dioxide from the use of any carbon-based fuel. The lack of alternatives to wood in many developing countries, or the limitations placed on agricultural productivity by the absence of cheap energy, also have damaging ecological consequences. In the wake of the oil-price rises of the 1970s, we face a world in which oil and gas are running out, nuclear power has turned out to be problematic and the use of coal is constrained by the adverse environmental impacts of its extraction and burning. What solutions to these very real problems are currently being investigated?

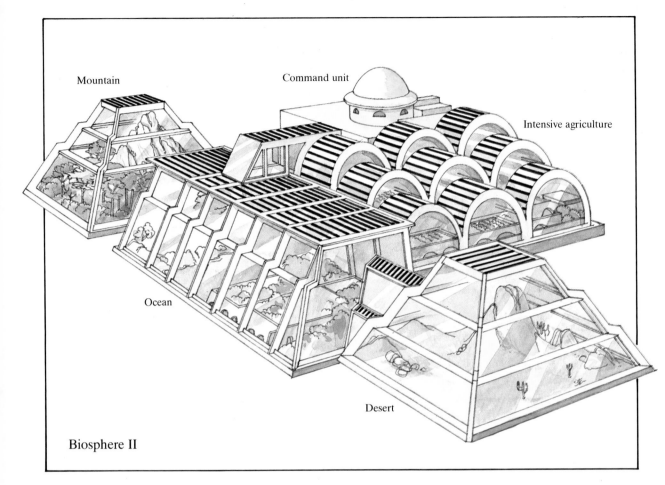

Mountain

Command unit

Intensive agriculture

Ocean

Desert

Biosphere II

One idea being given serious consideration is the "autonomous eco-house," which is totally self-contained, relies entirely upon ambient energy sources and recycles all its own waste. Small solar heaters, windmills, water wheels or methane digesters would provide the power needed by such small communities, which would concentrate on producing their own food supply and satisfying their own biological and social needs. An even more specialized, self-enclosed, self-sustaining environment is being constructed in the Catalina Mountains, 35 miles northeast of Tuscon, Arizona. *Biosphere II*, as it is called, will stretch over 9,700 square feet and will contain a rain forest, a swamp, a desert, an ocean and a vegetable garden. It will be powered solely by the sun's rays, which will be converted into electricial energy. Constructed to house a two-year experiment, *Biosphere II* may well provide important clues about how feasible it will be for humans to

This is a model of Biosphere II, *showing its constituent environments. It will be possible to isolate the different modules from each other, thus forming a number of self-contained eco-systems.*

The emphasis on conservation would create a great diversity of jobs, unskilled as well as skilled, in thousands of factories and work-shops across the country – in sharp contrast to the specialized, centralized and limited job opportunities implied by the conventional supply-expansion energy forecasts and policies. If the major energy-using countries followed a similar path, the effects on global development and confidence in the future would be extraordinary.

G. Leach: A Low Energy Strategy for the United Kingdom

recreate a "natural" self-sufficient environment by constructing an artificial living unit. Is this a glimpse of the future today?

Such a system, however, would require revolutionary changes in our way of life. Do most people want to give up their urban lifestyle in favor of these kinds of rural and artificial living spaces? It could be argued that the advocates of alternative technology and small-scale eco-units are confusing potential problems that may be raised by a decline in some energy resources, with those caused by the "misuse" of urban institutions.

The ideas of the alternative technologists resemble in large measure those of the Green Party and other ecology groups who detest what they regard as the ruthless exploitation of the world's resources. They fear that modern society's obsession with industrialization and urbanization will destroy the world as we know it. One obvious example, they would claim, is the rate at which the world's equatorial forest is being felled. This action not only endangers the very existence of thousands of species of animals and plants, but threatens to upset the world's climatic balance. These great forests produce much-needed carbohydrates, oxygen and water vapor. The equatorial sun's great heat causes thermals to develop, cloud formation and heavy rainfall.

Those who advocate the use of alternative technology fear that, in our ever more sophisticated attempts to follow the illusion of "progress," we are becoming more and more "denaturalized" – separated from our natural environment and alienated from our role in it and our responsibility to it. They argue that this process, which began with the Industrial Revolution, is getting increasingly out of our control and that we refuse to face or understand its consequences. Should we educate ourselves to think differently about our lifestyles or are these notions the result of an idealized view of nature and our relationship to it? Will we be forced to re-create nature, as in *Biosphere II*, in order to return to a more "natural" way of life?

The world's forests, including this one in Sri Lanka, are being destroyed for timber or to provide more land for agriculture.

5 Attitudes to energy

The future is a cause of constant controversy. Pessimists believe that the world is about to enter upon a period of energy shortage, when standards of living must necessarily fall. Optimists are confident that scientists will discover new means of tapping the resources of the sun, hot rocks, the wind, the ocean, and oil shale and tar sand deposits – these renewables and fossil fuels offer a potent source of hope. As energy pressures continue to intensify, they argue, planners will take a fresh look at some of the old sources of energy, as well as developing wholly new technologies.

By combining design concepts that have been known for centuries with modern building materials, we can now build houses that even in the coldest climates receive 75–90 percent of their energy from the sun. Simple solar collectors are now to be found heating water in over two million Japanese buildings and, within ten years, the Japanese expect a third of their buildings to be equipped in this way. Sixty companies in twenty countries are now producing photovoltaic cells, which convert sunlight directly into electricity. Water pumps in Tunisia, electronic calculators in Europe, medical refrigerators in Africa and telecommunications systems in Papua New Guinea are now all powered by photovoltaic electricity. By the middle of the next century, as much as one-third of the world's electricity could come from the sun.

Unfortunately most governments still regard renewable energy as the Cinderella of energy policy, to be considered, if at all, only as an afterthought. However, a substantial shift of

Left An artist's impression of a small rural community in the twenty-first century that relies entirely on renewable energy sources.

financial, intellectual and administrative resources in favor of the renewables would strengthen both the economy (by ensuring adequate supplies of energy) and the environment (by reducing the ecological stresses of energy use).

We must conserve as much energy as we can by storage and by recycling waste products. Cheap energy created very wasteful habits. Now that energy is expensive, ways to get the most of every source used are being developed. This not only creates a cleaner and healthier environment, it also reduces costs for industry. We must do even more to prevent the health of the planet being endangered by the build up of toxic concentrations of carbon dioxide and heavy metals in the air, by the destruction of the equatorial forests and by accidents at our nuclear power stations. In the Developing World, wasteful use of energy must also be eliminated. Scarce and expensive wood is inefficiently burned and animal power is poorly utilized (e.g. through poor harnessing, and through inefficient farming equipment).

People's ideas about energy are often mixed up with their beliefs about human society. Some fear that we are embarking on a course leading to excessive urbanization, mechanization and centralization. They conclude we shall become dehumanized in some great space-age empire. Such people call for a return to what they regard as simpler, superior lifestyles, such as small-scale, semi-independent settlements where people are self-sufficient and make important decisions for themselves while remaining close to the land and nature. However, urbanization does not necessarily lead to a decline in the quality of life. Nor does rural living automatically result in a utopia.

Human beings only emerged from the Stone Age a few thousand years ago. Since then, they have achieved many thrilling artistic, social, scientific and technological triumphs. They have also destroyed each other, damaged much of the land and animal and plant life and carried disease, waste and destruction wherever they have gone. It could be argued that the crisis facing humankind is not one of energy production, but of the kind of life we want to live. Energy sources must remain our servants and not become our masters.

Glossary

Ambient   Of, or relating to, the immediate surroundings.

Autonomous   Self-sufficient and self-supporting.

Atom   The smallest unit of a chemical element.

Carbohydrates   Energy-producing food that is present in green plants.

China Syndrome   A total meltdown of the core of a nuclear reactor, which burns its way through the earth's crust. The term arises from the theory that the core could burn straight through from one side of the earth to the other, e.g. from the U.S. to China.

Core   The part of a nuclear reactor containing the fuel.

Developed World   The rich, industrialized countries of North America, Europe, the U.S.S.R., Japan, Australia and New Zealand.

Developing World   The poorer countries of Asia, Africa and Latin America.

Eco-unit   A self-supporting living environment.

Ecosystem   A system involving the interactions between a community and its non-living environment.

Ecology   The study of the relationships between living organisms and their environment.

Electricity   A form of energy arising from the movement of electrons through a conductor.

Energy   The capacity to do work.

Fission   The splitting of an atom into two or more fragments.

Fossil fuels   Fossilized organic matter (plants, animals, etc) in the form of oil, natural gas and coal.

Fusion   The joining of two atomic nuclei to form a single nucleus.

Geothermal energy   Heat emanating from the earth's core.

Graphite   A crystalline carbon used as a moderator in nuclear reactors.

Heat exchanges   A device that transfer heat from one fluid to another without allowing them to mix.

Hydroelectricity   Electricity generated by water power.

Hydrogen   The lightest element.

Kinetic energy   Energy that an object has because it is moving.

Meltdown   The melting of the core of a nuclear reactor, caused when the reaction has gone out of control. The heat generated by this is so intense that the core could burn its way through the earth's crust, releasing harmful radiation into the water, soil and rocks.

Neutron   A tiny uncharged particle found in an atom's nucleus.

Oil shale   A type of rock from which crude oil can be extracted.

OPEC   The Organization of Petroleum Exporting Countries that controls the production and cost of much of the world's oil.

Radioactivity   Nuclear particles and gamma radiation emitted when an atomic nucleus decays.

Renewables   Sources of energy that have a non-finite supply, e.g. wind, sun or tidal energy.

Reserves   The amount of a fuel substance stored in the earth.

Solar energy   Energy emitted by the sun.

Superconductor   A material that has an electrical resistance close to zero at very low temperatures.

Tar sands   Sandstone from which crude oil can be extracted.

Temperature inversion   A layer of cold air trapped below a layer of warmer air.

Turbine   A machine that converts the kinetic energy of a moving fluid (water, steam, etc) to mechanical energy by causing it to turn a bladed rotor.

Books to read

*More with Less: The Future World of Buck-
minister Fuller* by Nathan Aaseng (Lerner,
1986)
Feast or Famine: The Energy Future by
Franklyn M. Branley (Crowell, 1980)
The Coal Question by Bertha Davis & Susan
Whitfield (Watts, 1982)
Energy: Choices for the Future by Barbara R.
Fogel (Watts, 1985)
Sun Power: Facts about Solar Energy by Steve
Gadler & Wendy Adamson (Lerner, 1978)
The Greenhouse Effect by Kathlyn Gay
(Watts, 1986)
Acid Rain by Kathlyn Gay (Watts, 1983)
Geothermal Energy: A Hot Prospect by
Augusta Goldin (Harcourt, 1980)
*Oceans of Energy: Reservoir of Power for the
Future* by Augusta Goldin (Harcourt, 1980)
*Shale Oil and Tar Sands: The Promises and
Pitfalls* by Richard B. Lyttle (Watts, 1982)
Energy Isn't Easy by Norman F. Smith (Cow-
ard-McCann, 1981)
The Nuclear Question by Ann Weiss (Har-
court, 1981)

Other References
North-South: A Programme for Survival. Inde-
pendent Commission of Internaitonal
Development Issues (MIT Press, 1980)
*North-South, Common Crisis: Cooperation for
World Recovery.* Independent Comission
of Internaitonal Development Issues (MIT
Press, 1983)

Picture Acknowledgments

ACE Photo Agency 31 (left); Bryan & Cherry Alexander 29; Camera Press 6, 20, 21, 28; Bruce Coleman
25, 38, 41; Mary Evans 9; Hutchinson 15, 33, 37; Richard McBride Photography frontispiece, 7, 11, 34; Shell
cover, 16, 23; ZEFA 8, 13, 14, 17, 26, 27, 31, 32, 39, 47; Greenpeace 20; Artwork by Malcolm Walker.

Index

Opposite *Coal-fired power station at Didcot, England.*